BOLD
ageless

WINTER 2018

ON THE COVER
SHERIE YVETTE
WITHERS-BANKS

Industreetwithtinabandmroutley
Tuesday
6-8pm
STATUS NETWORK
MEDIA - BROADCASTING - PROMOTIONS

TABLE OF CONTENTS

WINTER 2018

COVER STORY

CEO
Lynita Mitchell-Blackwell

President
David M. Good

Editor-In-Chief
Tina Bridges

Associate Editor
Antoinette Melvin

Public Relations Director
Tinzley Bradford

Social Media Manager
Christine Adams

Creative Director
Courtney Monday

Photography
Ynette Keith

Videography
Toyin Fadina

Distribution PMD, Inc.
Arthur Pope

OUR CONTRIBUTORS
WINTER 2018

Harold Outley

Brenda L. Dubone

Nissa K

Tiny Gardner

Bj Bowman

Lanita Jo Fox

Jules Johnson

SET LIFE

When you are learning the ropes to acting, there is no 1 road to travel to be successful. There are MANY!!! When you decide to work as an EXTRA on set, please be mindful of ALL set etiquette. If you are new to this and find yourself full of unanswered questions, but you do not know the chain of command. (Who to speak with) Please learn the difference between Set P.A., P.A., Office P. A., A. D., 1st A. D., 2nd A. D., 2nd 2nd, Director, script supervisor, etc etc. Before you attempt to approach anyone, ask your fellow background actors. Never, and I do mean Never go up to the Director to ask anything. This is the quickest way to get Black Balled!!! Meaning it will become extremely difficult to get work as background, you may not get anymore work. So be mindful and aware of who you ask questions on set!!!

HAPPY ACTING & SEE YOU ON SET!!!

Brenda L Dubone

TNT ENTERTAINMENT PRESENTS

2ND ANNUAL

Women
OF HONOR
AWARDS 2019

SUNDAY, FEBRUARY 10TH, 2019

RENDEZVOUS EVENT CENTER
4717 JONESBORO ROAD
FOREST PARK, GA 30297
5:00PM-8:00PM | $25 ADMISSION

HOSTED BY
Tribel & Tina

MEN OF HONOR
AWARDS

2018 HONOREES

Brian Jordan
Mayor Vince Williams
Len Gibson
Christopher Martin
Ben Norman
Bobby Peoples

Earnest Moore
James "JB" Brown
Zeus Luby
Christopher Emanuel
Marvin Arrington Jr.

Dr. Ron Williamson
Eric Thomas
Jack Tre
Donald Craddock
Bryant K. Marshall
Will Rivers

WORDS UNSPOKEN
The Letter

Amazing how things come full circle after examining our journey from the beginning stages ...
Collectively and individually we've grown, at different rates, often times on different pages ...
But the love for one another became contagious ...
Going through a plethora of phases unsure whether we'd make it ...
Our willingness to fight for us is what saved it ...
despite the breaks in between ... dating others, as if we were REALLY done ... simply faking it ...
You're the one ... You're MY one, always HAVE been ...
Excuse my tardiness since I was the LAST to know ...
More than my greatest love ... my grand finale ... my encore ... my curtain call
After my heavenly Father you come before all ... and NOW look at us ...
We're here ...
Can you believe we've finally made it??!!!
All the stress, flowers, guest lists, dresses and more ... Our moment
Let's OWN it ... Only the beginning ... brightest days lie ahead
I'm so tired right now really just wanna get in our bed
But instead
I'm ... watching my angel walk down that aisle ...
Holding back a river full of tears ... smiling incredibly on the inside
Been here before but no expiration date this time around
Cheers to you my Queen ... lt's my honor to OFFICIALLY bestow upon you ... YOUR crown ... I love you ...

With eternal love
YOUR King
Harold E. Outley ©2017

Lessons within Good and Bad

.... 93% of all situations have something good that can be found within them. Yes, the bad ones also. Stop letting those bad ones bring you down.

Yes ... I do understand that there is an initial reaction to a bad situation, but you have to keep it a reaction. Do not let a reaction consume you to the point that it becomes a reality. Do not let it continue to sit in your space. Use it -learn from it, you can share it .... as it might help another.

Think about it -if a good situation/blessing comes about, it can be detrimental to you if not used correctly. So use the bad ones as well as the good ones. There is a reason for every situation/incident in life -it is up to you to learn from them, and to use them the right way.

#aKlassicMansBelief

Blinded by the Want

.... sometimes you can want something so Badly that you find yourself chasing the good in the situation. While within the chase, you can become blinded to some of the bad that could be. It is so easy to find yourself acting out of character to get what you want - when it is probably something you really do not need.

Stay within yourself, stay true to yourself -open your eyes, and pay attention as you chase what you want. Some things that you want, that you think you may need --- just are not in God's plans for you!

Recognize it so that you can get back to what God has in store for you

AND THE WINNER IS...

REPYOURACT ACTORS COMPETITION KIDS AND ADULT WINNER RON EDWARDS AND PATIENCE ROZIER

Ronald Edwards was in born in Philadelphia, PA and later moved to Thomasville, GA and while there he studied advanced drama courses in high school under the direction of Fred Allen who was also a Professor of Julliard Arts Institution. Ron was a natural and began to compete in "One Act Play" for various productions such as "Death of A Salesman" and "Raisin In The Sun". Ronald has always been musically inclined too! At the mere age of 9 years old he began to play the piano in church by ear. He then discovered he could play the drums very well and was a percussionist in his high school marching band. He began to play in his local church faithfully and then played the piano for various churches and gospel choirs around the world. Ron has conducted and directed several gospel concerts in Germany during the 23 years that he served in the United States Army.

While serving in the military Ron was deployed several times to Baghdad, Afghanistan, Iraq, and Bosnia. While he was away from home he decided to write gospel stage plays and songs to keep his mind off of what was going on around him. A few gospel plays Ron has written are entitled " I Need You Now", "The Rough Side of The Mountain", and a gospel comedy "Pop Jenkins: Family Matters".

Ron has always desired to be in theatre and movies. Acting is truly not just a gift and talent to him but it's his passion that he has for the arts. He would love to teach and inspire the youth that have a desire to act as well and one day will open up a School of Music and Theatre. Ronald travels weekly to Atlanta, GA pursuing his acting career. His positive energy and comedic, charismatic personality will definitely leave you speechless and wanting to see more on the stage and on the big screen! Ron now resides in Columbus, GA and where he is married to his lovely wife and high school sweetheart of 21 years Kimi Edwards. They have 3 beautiful children Maya Edwards, Kimani Edwards, and Myles Edwards.

PATIENCE ROZIER

Patience Rozier is a 15-year-old actress in Atlanta. Her first theatrical role was as contestant host-Contesta in the 2013 Studio of the Arts production of Miss Personality. She later played the roles of Death in His Majesty's Secret Service (2014), Nikki Fury in the 2015 production of The Forgettables and Madame de la Grande Bouche in Twin Rivers Middle School 2017 production of Beauty and the Beast Jr. Last summer she played the role of Ed in The Lion King Jr. at the Aurora Theatre in Lawrenceville, GA, and Ruth Jones in the web series The Midlife.

This summer she played the role of Charlie Bucket in the Aurora Theatre's production of Willy Wonka Jr. Other roles include Carter in the short film Selfless: True Happiness, and Seraph in the TPN short film Temporary Darkness. Patience played Umara in the award winning short film Noise, written by Damn Write Original's Nakia Stevens. She was recently nominated and won Best Breakout Actress at the 2017 TPN Awards for her role as Charity in the short film CDs. Patience has been dancing since the age of 3 and has experience in both Modem and Tap. She is an avid reader who plays the ukulele, keyboard, and flute in her spare time, and is currently writing her first novel.

She studies theatre and film with HOTT Theater for Children in Smyrna under the amazing Lauren Hunt and is represented by TDH Talent Agency in Lawrencville, GA.

I did not know what telomeres were until June 2016. As we age, and yes we are going to do that our telomere shortens. They can weaken due to stress, and just everyday life. I take them every day, and I can see the difference in my body. Telomerase counteracts telomere shortening. An enzyme named telomerase adds bases to the ends of telomeres. In young cells, telomerase keeps telomeres from wearing down too much. But as cells divide repeatedly, there is not enough telomerase, so the telomeres grow shorter and the cells age.Telomeres, repetitive TTAGGG) DNA-protein complexes at the ends of chromosomes, are crucial for the survival of cancer cells. They are maintained by an enzyme called telomerase in the vast majority of tumors . ... Telomeres protect chromosome ends from fusion and from being recognized as sites of DNA damage. Telomeres are the caps at the end of each strand of DNA that protect our chromosomes, like the plastic tips at the end of shoelaces. Without the coating, shoelaces become frayed until they can no longer do their job, just as without telomeres, DNA strands become damaged and our cells can't do their job.

LaNita Jo Fox

lanitajoe.isagenix.com
Feel Like A Million
Get Fit to Live
atinal.com

#TLASIGHTINGPARIS

beautiful designs by Norahs Khan the models of TLA looked amazing and had a wonderful time enjoying the sights of Paris

JE T'AIME
CMG
PARIS FW

We've Only Just Begun To Live

James Alvin West & DeEtta (Little) West

We met on a BLIND DATE! Prior to this moment my husband had participated in the wedding of Bill and Debra where he in the aftermath had approached Debra about being introduced to one of the many women at their Reception. Debra told James that "you don't want any of the women at this wedding". She stated that I have someone for you that you would love (Debra previously had established a credible relationship with DeEtta where she felt she could speak in this manner). A short time had passed by and the date and time was set. We met on March 9, 1979 . This date became the day of "New Beginnings." Our first date took place at the home Debra & Bill. Per my husband's description……"The entrance was made of the beautiful lady" and for James it was love at first sight.For DeEtta it was friendship at first sight. Love came two years after the marriage. The evening progressed and was accentuated by both desiring to meet again to explore a possible relationship. James conveyed his desire for the relationship to be established not based on sex. Somewhat surprised by the statement I said ok but admitted later to him that his request for us to abstain from having sex in the courtship was one of my 3 basic require-

ments. That following Sunday became the next time that the two of us connected, which was at my sister's apartment where I was living at the time. That was when James met my/our daughter, who was 2 years old at the time. The relationship took off on that day and we never looked back.

On May 4, 1979 at 9:30pm at a traffic light/intersect in Marino Del Rey, California James said "let's get married" and DeEtta said "ok". The date was set for July 7th of that year. Yes James proposed to me after two months and then married me two months later. Our wedding took place at The Park Windsor Baptist Church where James served as Associate Pastor. The Church family came together under the grateful leadership of Manuel Scott Jr., who performed the ceremony, and new life had begun.

 Three and a half months after meeting, new beginnings, two wonderful grand-children, three happy and productive children (grownups) and almost 40 years later we're still experiencing 'new beginnings', we're still trying to make it work and we know that God is the glue that keeps us bond together.

SHERIE YVETTE WITHERS-BANKS

Sherie Yvette Withers-Banks

Professional Model and Whitney Houston tribute artist

My makeup glam squad: Marcus Geeter and Landis of Landis Cosmetics

D .0.8. 12/17/66

Married to Anthony T. Banks (10 years)
Parents: Mr. and Mrs. William Withers Jr. (53 years married)

Sibling: Jihad Salahuddin- my kidney transplant donor
(7/19/2005)

Lupus Nephritis survivor- 20 years
Kidney transplant - 13 year ago
Member of ''Living Life with Lupus Support Group''(1998-present)

Graduated 1991 Chicago State University
Bachelor of Science Degree in Dietetics Ful Full time Nutritionist
@ Chicago Family Health Center (1991-Present)

Member of St John De La Sal le parish

Volunteer Entertainer for the:
South Central programs and services Puttn' on the Hits lip-sync dinner fundraiser. My great friend and director Felicia Blasingame is also a board member and mentor

(May 2018) 1st place lip -sync contest Winner as ''Whitney''

Sherie Yvette is a Professional model and ''Whitney Houston'' look-alike-Tribute Artist

1987: Finished Professional Model training at the only black owned/operated Modeling/Charm school in the Chatham area Cleo Johnson Modeling School

As a Professional Model

Titles Won: Miss Windy C'ity 1991 & MS. Windy City 1999

TV /Commercials: Andriana Furs, Saxon Paint, (hand model) for Wrigley Gum, Room Place furniture

Publications/Print: Billboard for Namaste/Organic Root Stimulator hair company, Leisure Curl Hair Ad, Coca-Cola, American Girl, Ebony Magazine, Sophisticate's Black Hair, Y.K. International wig catalog, Ladies Home Journal, L'Amour Bridal, N'Digo, ORS (Organic Root Stimulator, Soft Sheen, etc.

Trade Shows: Proud Lady Beauty Show & Midwest Beauty Show (Chicago). Bronner Bros. Hair Show (Atlanta), Orlando Premier Hair show (Orlando, Fl) : Namaste/Organic Root Stimulator, Revlon, Avlon, Soft Sheen, Johnsons1 Elente and Mizani, Black Expo & Todays Black Woman Expo, N'DIGO GALA, Night of 100 Stars, Chicago Auto Show, etc.

Runway: BET fashion show, Essence Magazine Mall Celebrity fashion show, United Negro College Fund (UNCF)1 National Cosmeto·logy Association, Bridal Expo Shows, Cook County Bar association, Sorority/Fraternity Convention events, Empress/ Majestic Star/Trump Casino corporate events, Carsons/ Macy' /BeBe/Talbots fashion shows, etc

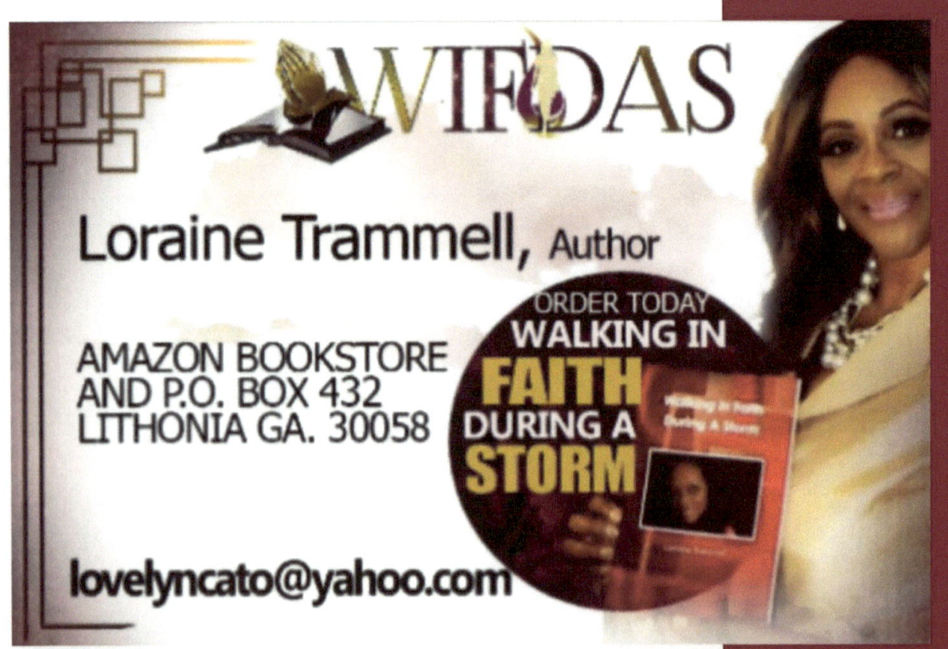

WIFDAS
Loraine Trammell, Author
AMAZON BOOKSTORE
AND P.O. BOX 432
LITHONIA GA. 30058
lovelyncato@yahoo.com
ORDER TODAY
WALKING IN
FAITH
DURING A
STORM

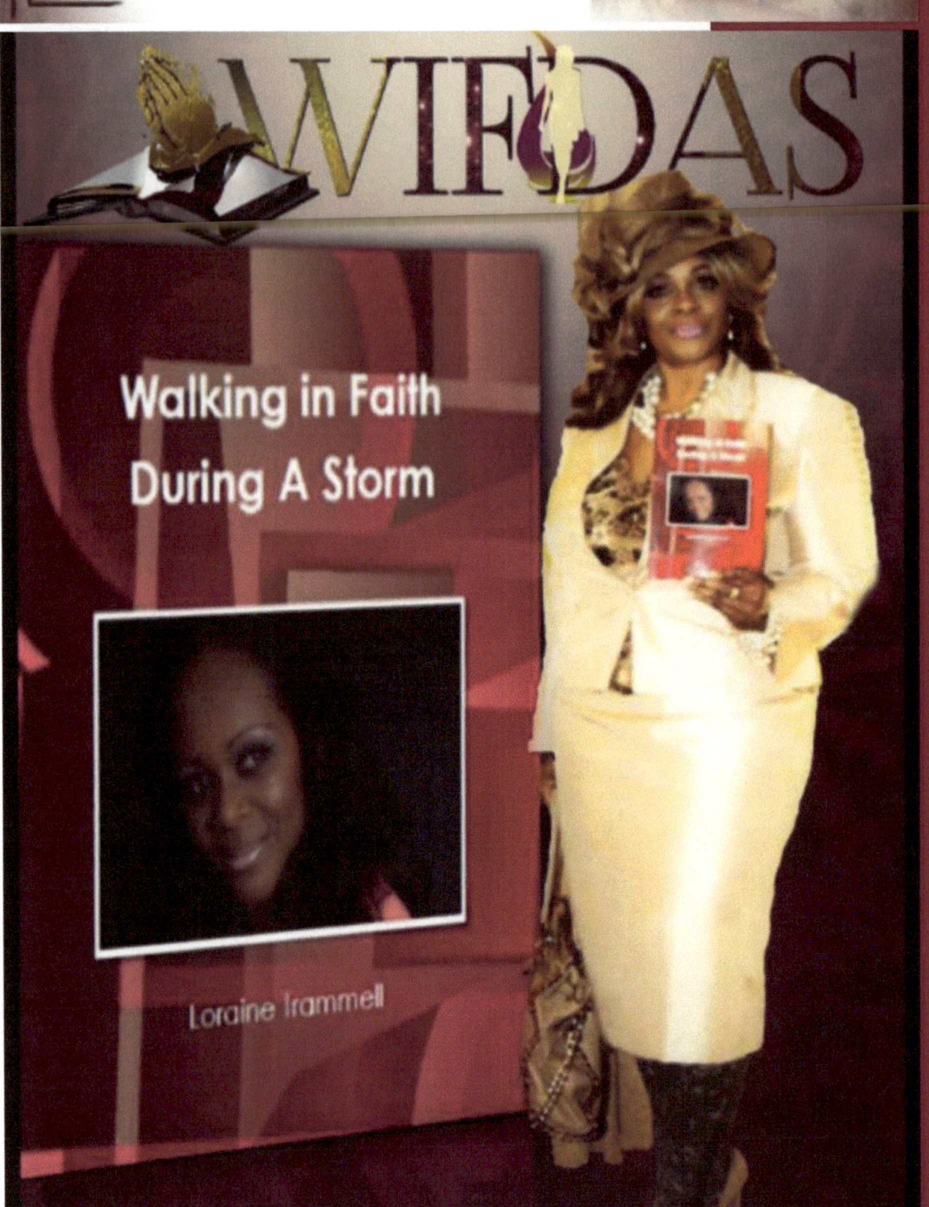

WIFDAS
Walking in Faith
During A Storm
Loraine Trammell

MAURICE
THOMPSON
#BEINGAGELESS

Food
For
Thought

Food for thought ..... Your belief factor plays a significant role in your everyday life. Your attitude, what u think, say and do are all a reflection of what u believe. Everything that you're believing in God for is right there in front of u waiting on u to start walking in it. What are u waiting on? Amen!

#MinisterBJ

TINY'S CORNER

1 What do
you call an fat
zombie?

A: Dead weight

2 A man walks in a barber
shop and ask for a shag,
and have a big patch cut
out of his head, the barber
replies why you want me
to do that?

*A: The man says I don't but you
cut it it like that last time....*

3 What do you name
a pig on fire ?

A: Crispy Bacon

#REPYOURACT

2nd annual the venue was amazing with a huge auditorium and the entertainement was awesome, talented judges host by James Thompson and red carpet host by Brenda Dubone. Founder and creator Lauren Hunt did a spectacular job once again.

Soft Hues
PHOTOGRAPHY
TLB
Productions
gs Media
Sunny
angs
By

REP YOUR ACT WINNERS

Eat
&
Drink
With
Me

Divine Visions Catering:

I found out about this company
via social media. I am a rideshare
driver and a fellow driver made
a post that he was picking up his
meals for the week and how much
he loved the food.

He started describing the process and let us know that the point of contact (Wanda Miller) is also a ride-share driver so it was really easy for us to connect with her. I initiated contact, was blessed to get a 3-course meal tasting setup with Wanda, Marketing/Delivery Executive and Executive ChefDunn and the rest is the lovely foodie present and tasty future. I enjoyed the following:

- Summer Salad - mixed greens and cranberries
- Greek Salad - cucumbers, feta, red onion with balsamic vinegarette
- Pesto Angel Hair Pasta

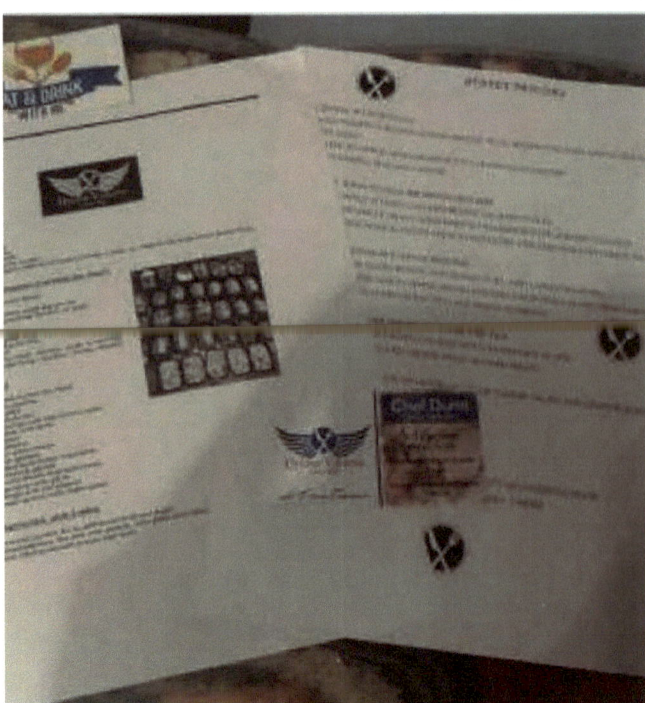

Divine Visions Catering is a catering company that handles ALL events and festivities AND they also do meal planning. Chef Dunn hails from Cleveland Ohio and has been tantalizing taste buds for over 10 years. I have signed up for their meal planning services, there are several different levels from individual meal purchase up to a 30-day subscription. Each time a customer chooses the plan , they have the choice of

proteins and vegetables and an all vegetable option.

I contacted Wanda, made my payment and my meals were delivered to my home. I chose the 5 meals for the week plan. I chose turkey meatloaf, salmon and grilled chicken for my three proteins and string beans and rice for my two veggies. I was a happy camper, everything is already freshly cooked and delivered in awesome containers which can be saved and used later. All I had to do was warm it up and eat!

All of the food that I experienced was delicious! The customer service impeccable! Everything is freshly

cooked, every week, gotta love it!

Make sure that you are following Divine Visions Catering on social media and visit their website to read more about Chef Dunn and his cooking adventures. Inbox Wanda Miller if you are interested in joining the meal plan customer base and she will get you taken care of.

Their catering services start from an private, intimate meal for 1 to any family or Corporate crowd, sit down or buffet style dining! They also provide cooking demos, which is always a fun group event. Visit their site soon to setup your event, you will not regret it! I look forward to picking out my ingredients for the week! I am definitely a fan, trust me you will be too! TIDS is the catering compan)' for your next event, Divine Visions Catering.

[overall] Score: 10

Hours of operation: By Appointment
Divine Visions Catering
Sandy springs, GA
(678) 224-1538
www.divinevisionscatering.com

Keep up with foodie events in Atlanta and surrounding cities, follow our FB page-· Eat And Drink With Me
~Follow~
Instagram. com/EatAnDrink WithMe
Face book. coin/ eatandrinkwithn1e
Tvvitter.com/eatnd1inkwithme

EatanDrinkWithMe. wix.com/eatandrinkwithme
#EADWM
#dineandreview

Photography by: Nissa K
Review by: Nissa K

Please leave coniments. Would you like to arrange a food review for your eatery? This food blogger can be reached via email at: eatandrinlovith111e@ gn1ail.com

~Are you a female blogger? Are you a female working in the arts? Check out these support organizations: Women With Gifts Bold Favor Magazine~

Website:
www.eatandrinkwithme.wix.com/eatandrinkwithme
www.divinevisionscatering.com

Talented, upcoming actor/producer Lester Greene is on the rise having worked with notable directors Phil Allocco, Eric McGinty and Ben Baker. He has also had the opportunity to work with heavy hitters 50 Cent and Omari Hardwick.

Greene starred in and produced two short films: "Driving Force" and "Raw Footage;' both of which aired on CBS (with Antoine Allen & Emelyn Stuart). He also produced two other short films, "I Got a Callback;' and "The Last Fishing Trip" with filmmaker Christopher Fox.

He majored in English/ Journalism at Queens College, and he studied with the likes of Alec Baldwin (Southampton Theatre Conference), Peter Miner (Terry Schreiber Studios), Matt Newton, Mary Boyer and David Goldberg (Edge Studio). He won best actor for his role in "Driving Force" at the Atlantic City Cinefest Downbeach Film Festival, and he won the Actors' Showdown Monologue Competition at the Las Vegas Black Film Festival.

Greene landed several speaking roles on Gotham, Power, Jon Glaser Loves Gear, 50 Central, Luckiest Guys on the Lower East Side, I Am Homicide and Rachael Ray. He has also appeared in various commercials for Chase, Rogaine, AAO, FYI, Amazon, MTB Bank, Citizen Watch, Peeps Delights, Buzzfeed, Boost Mobile, Crown Royal, Brooks, and many more. He has four rap albums on I-tunes: "The Greenehouse Effect;' "Cocktails;' "No Bush, Straight Dicks" and "The Greene Room."

Jules Johnson, stepped out on faith and launched her own small business, NOBLE, a natural body care product line.

In a society where we are taught to go to school and go work, that becomes all that we know, we become attached to a job but what about turning our own dream s into reality; and that is just what I did. It wasn't an easy decision, however I knew that I couldn't truly build a business while building someone else's.

Working since I was 15 years old has taught me A LOT and those experiences can never be devalued just because I worked for others. We all have our own paths, and sometimes on these paths there are many twists and turns before your find a clearing. I would tell any one who is thinking of starting their own business is first, take advice without allowing your feelings to be hurt. Secondly, be flexible; sometimes our way isn't the best, or most cost effective way, so know when to be flexible but still be clear and firm about your vision. Thirdly, don't be afraid to seek out help. For me I needed help with the creative steps, and my Creative Consultant has been amazing, but I needed help from someone who owned that area, and she does. And finally, be patient and passionate! Nothing happens over night and there will be growing pains, but if you are passionate about your product or service, let that fuel you through those tough days and long nights.

Jules Johnson
Motto
-Nourish Your Body
With Nature!

COVER GIRL CONTESTANTS

SHARON GARY DILL HACKNEY

SYVIA OMO ABU

LANITA JO FOX

SONTA KERR

SHERIE YVETTE WITHERS

AMBER LYONS

MARIE RICHARDS

NNISSA ELLIOTT

TONYA PARRISH

ERIKA FOCSIMAMA PARKER

LORAINE TRAMMELL

BRENDA CURRY TURNER

BRENDA DUBONE

TONJALERRA SLEDGE HARRIS

KAVON HILL

LAKEEBA WALLACE

Brenda Curry-Turner
5'7 size2 @bren1bren83
UBER LOVE
2ND ANNUAL
Women
OF HONOR
AWARDS 2019
2019
HONOREES
SUNDAY, FEBRUARY 10TH, 2019
RENDEZVOUS EVENT CENTER
4717 JONESBORO ROAD FOREST PARK GA 30297
WRITTEN, PRODUCE, DIRECTED BY TINA B
#TLBPRODUCTIONS
Indstreet with tina b and mr outley
Tuesday 6-8pm
SHe
SAID
VOTE
TLB

MODELS
OVER 40

1. Sonta Kerr
2. Tenaya Peters
3. Tonya Parrish
4. Juaketha Lewis

5. Simone Jenkins
6. Angelia Allison

7. Nnissa Elliott
8. Tonjalerra Harris

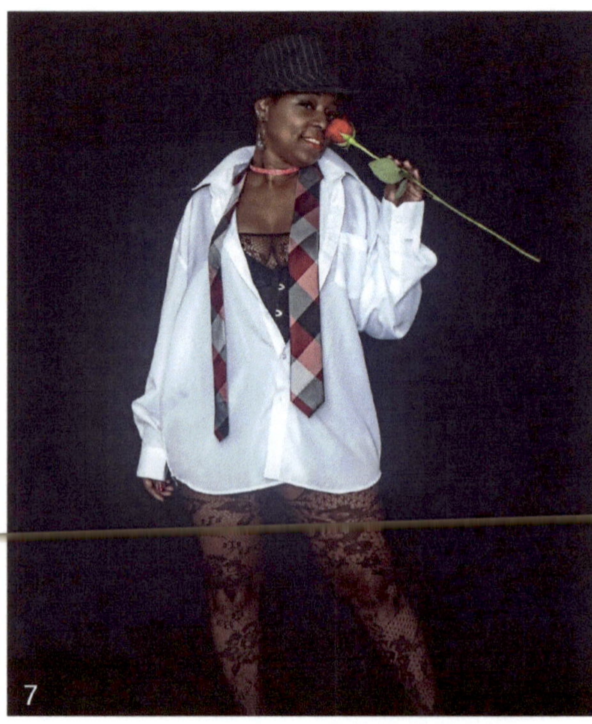

9. Deanna Bell
10. Charisse Ramey

11. Monetia Smothers
12. Bj Bowman

9

11

10

12

MODELS
OVER 50

1. Joyce White
2. Jonice Cromartie
3. Beth Crady
4. Roxanne Grimsley

5. James Thompson
6. Brenda Curry Turner

7. Saundra Owens Whitmore
8. Saberina Wilson

1. Barbara Moore
2. Lanita Jo Fox
3. Francine Stuart

Industreetwithtinabandmroutley
STATUS NETWORK
Media - Broadcasting - Promotions
every
Tuesday
6-8pm